JAMES NIXON

Raintree is an imprint of Capstone Global Library Limited, a company incorporated in England and Wales having its registered office at 264 Banbury Road, Oxford, OX2 7DY – Registered company number: 6695582

www.raintree.co.uk
myorders@raintree.co.uk

Edited by James Nixon
Designed by Keith Williams, sprout.uk.com
Picture Research by James Nixon
Production by Discovery Books
Originated by Capstone Global Library Limited
Printed and bound in India

ISBN 978 1 4747 5897 0 (hardback)
22 21 20 19 18
10 9 8 7 6 5 4 3 2 1

ISBN 978 1 4747 5901 4 (paperback)
23 22 21 20 19
10 9 8 7 6 5 4 3 2 1

British Library Cataloguing in Publication Data
A full catalogue record for this book is available from the British Library.

Acknowledgements
We would like to thank the following for permission to reproduce photographs:
Cover image (Roman Babakin/Shutterstock); Alamy: pp. 6 (Stewart Smith), 17 (Bob Gibbons), 22 (Michael Olivers), 23 (LowePhoto), 24 (Patrick Ward), 25 (Ashley Cooper); Shutterstock: pp. 4 (Duncan Andison), 5 (Cartarium), 8 (patjo), 9 (Steve Allen), 10 (EddieCloud), 11 (witchcraft), 12 (Derek Young photography), 13 (Dave Wainwright), 14 (MJSquared Photography), 15 (Drew Rawcliffe), 16 (Swen Stroop), 18 (Mark Medcalf), 19 (Zhecho Planinski), 20 (Antony Cooper), 21 (Paul Nash), 27 (Duncan Andison), 28 (Brendan Howard), 29 (Joe Dunckley); Wikimedia: p. 7 (Adrian Pingstone).

We would like to thank Dr Gillian Fyfe for her invaluable help in the preparation of this book.

Contents

The shape of Britain **4**
How do mountains form? **6**
Types of valleys **10**
Britain's highest peaks **12**
Mountain wildlife **16**
Working in the mountains **20**
Training and rescue **24**
Mountain fun **26**
Map of the UK **30**
Glossary **31**
Find out more **32**
Index **32**

The shape of Britain

Large hills are called mountains. In Britain, a mountain is a **peak** that rises over 610 metres (2,000 feet) high. Between the hills and mountains, the land drops to form low areas called **valleys**. Valleys often have rivers running through them.

A view of mountains and valleys in England's Lake District.

Some areas of Britain are low and flat. But in most parts, the landscape rises to form small hills or larger mountains.

Nearly all of the UK's mountains are found in Scotland, Wales, Northern Ireland and northern England. In southern England, there are two small mountain tops on Dartmoor.

On this map of the UK, the highest mountains are shown in orange. The hills are shown in yellow.

How do mountains form?

Mountains take millions of years to form. You can't feel it, but parts of the Earth's surface are moving extremely slowly. These movements in the ground can squeeze rocks together and push them upwards. Over a long period of time, some rocks have formed sharp, jagged **peaks**.

An Teallach in the Scottish Highlands has a row of peaks that point up like sharp teeth.

A group of mountains close together is called a **range**. Some ranges in Britain were formed by **volcanoes** long ago. The Cuillin range is on the Isle of Skye in north-west Scotland. The Cuillin was formed by hot, **molten** rock rising up from the surface. The rock cooled and went hard to make these mountains.

The spectacular Cuillin range started to form around 60 million years ago.

Not all mountains are rocky and jagged. Older mountains are often rounded and smoother. They have been worn down over time by the rain, ice and strong winds. Water trapped in rocks can also turn to ice. This splits the rocks apart.

The smooth Cheviot Hills were formed around 400 million years ago.

Valleys are also formed by rock wearing away. Rainwater rushes off the steep mountains. The water loosens rock and soil. It slowly carves out the shape of valleys.

Waterfalls can form where softer rocks are worn away more quickly than surrounding harder rocks.

Pistyll Rhaeadr, North Wales

This massive waterfall has formed an arch in the rock about halfway up.

Types of valleys

Water finds the quickest possible way downhill. Loose stones and rocks in the water help carve out steep-sided **valleys**. These are called V-shaped valleys because they have the same shape as the letter V. Rivers in the valleys wind and bend around areas of hard rock.

Water rushes down a V-shaped valley in Snowdonia National Park.

A **glacier** is a massive sheet of ice. Many thousands of years ago, glaciers filled Britain's valleys. They formed where snow had fallen but not melted. The glaciers slid very slowly downhill. As the glaciers moved, they wore away the rock and made valleys wider. V-shaped valleys were turned into U-shaped valleys.

High Cup Nick is one of the most famous U-shaped valleys in Britain. It is in the north Pennines.

Britain's highest peaks

Britain's highest mountains are found in the Scottish Highlands. Here, there are well over 100 mountains of 1,000 metres (3,280 feet) or higher. The tallest mountain in Britain is Ben Nevis. It stands at 1,345 metres (4,411 feet) high. The top is a collapsed dome of an ancient **volcano**.

Over 100,000 visitors walk up to the top of Ben Nevis every year.

The Lake District in north-west England contains England's steepest and highest mountains. The biggest is Scafell Pike. Its **summit** is 978 metres (3,209 feet) above sea-level. Wales's tallest **peak** is even higher. Mount Snowdon in north Wales stands at 1,085 metres (3,560 feet) high.

Ridges of sharp rock lead up to the pointed summit of Mount Snowdon.

As you go further up a mountain, the air gets colder. Near the tops of the highest peaks, patches of snow can lie on the ground all year. The mighty Cairngorms **range** in the eastern Highlands is Britain's snowiest place. Here, snow falls on around 76 days in every year.

The snowy Cairngorms has five of the six highest mountains in the UK. The other is Ben Nevis.

The weather on mountains can change very quickly. Storms and snowy **blizzards** can whip up suddenly. When air blows over the mountains it cools down as it rises. This causes more clouds to form and more rain to fall.

Storm clouds form over the mountains in the Lake District. The Lake District is is one of the wettest places in Britain.

Mountain wildlife

There is little **vegetation** at the tops of the highest mountains. Trees and plants that need sunshine and warmth grow lower down in the **valleys**. A few plants have found ways to survive the harsh conditions on the mountain tops. Mosses cling to the rocks. They have tiny leaves to protect themselves against wind and frost.

Compared to the mountains, valleys are greener and contain more plants and trees.

Some plants find shelter among the rocks and crags. They are able to survive without much water or soil. The Norwegian mugwort is one of Britain's rarest plants. It is found on only three mountains in north-west Scotland. The mugwort's strong, thick roots hold it tight to the ground in the strongest winds.

The Norwegian mugwort can grow on stony ground where there is little protection.

Some animals manage to survive the cold winters in the mountains. Animals such as red deer, foxes, hares and voles have **adapted** for life there. Mountain hares graze on the mountain's vegetation. In winter, the hare's fur turns white to **camouflage** it in the snow.

This mountain hare is finding shelter in a snow hole.

Birds such as ravens and peregrine falcons nest high up on the cliff faces. Golden eagles soar on the mountain winds. These eagles are massive. They have **wingspans** nearly 2 metres (7 feet) long. Golden eagles can kill prey as large as young deer.

All of Britain's golden eagles live in Scotland at the moment.

Working in the mountains

People don't live high up on the mountains. The weather is often bad and travelling there is difficult. People usually settle in the **valleys**. Here, the land is less steep and the soil is **fertile**. Farmers can grow crops in the valleys. There is also more grass there for cattle and sheep to graze on.

Farms and villages lie in the valley of Swaledale in the Yorkshire Dales National Park.

Farmers can't grow crops on the mountain's poor, thin soils. But some farmers keep sheep that graze on the mountain's higher slopes. Hill farming is hard work. It is difficult when the weather is very cold and wet. Many small farms have now been **abandoned**. Some have been turned into holiday homes for tourists.

The hills on Dartmoor have been grazed by animals for thousands of years.

Some of Britain's mountains contain caves and tunnels carved out by underground rivers. Some caves have now become major tourist attractions. Tunnels have also been dug out by **miners** searching for valuable metals in the mountain's rocks. Long ago, miners dug out lead, copper, silver and gold.

The tunnels at the National Showcaves Centre in the Brecon Beacons were discovered in 1912.

A quarry is a pit on a mountainside. In a quarry, workers dig up rocks and stones to use as building materials. Quarries are noisy places. Rock is blasted off the mountain using **explosives**. Every day, huge dump trucks take thousands of tons of rubble away.

Workers at quarries drive big diggers and trucks to move rocks and stones.

Training and rescue

The army use some mountains to train for fitness or battle. The tough **terrain** tests soldiers to their limits. Pen y Fan is the highest **peak** in the Brecon Beacons. Soldiers march across Pen y Fan carrying heavy backpacks. The gruelling course is 15 miles (24 kilometres) long.

Army trainees climb the steep path to the top of Pen y Fan.

Every mountainous region of Britain has its own mountain rescue team. A team is called out by the police if someone is lost or injured in the mountains. Team members are volunteers, but they are well trained. They carry ropes and stretchers. Rescue teams use helicopters so they can find people and take them to hospital quickly.

A member of a Lake District mountain rescue team gets ready to jump out of the helicopter.

Mountain fun

The mountains have become popular tourist **destinations**. The beautiful scenery and wildlife attracts many walkers. They enjoy the fresh air and a chance to explore. Mountain bikers like the adventure of cycling over steep, rocky trails.

A mountain biker bumps down some rocky steps in the Peak District.

Walkers love to reach the tops of mountains. But a few mountains are so craggy that they need to be **scrambled** up, or climbed with ropes. Climbers are well prepared and carry lots of safety equipment. Some people enjoy climbing or **abseiling** down cliff faces just for the thrill of it.

Scramblers use their hands as well as feet to climb mountains.

Mountains are great places for other extreme sports. **Paragliders** jump off mountains and soar like birds. Skiers and snowboarders rush down snow-covered slopes. The Scottish Highlands is home to five ski **resorts**. At these resorts, chairlifts give skiers a ride back up to the top.

The Glenshee Ski Centre on the edge of the Cairngorms National Park is Britain's largest ski resort.

On Cairn Gorm mountain, a tram-like vehicle takes skiers and tourists on a trip almost 1,100 metres (3,600 feet) up the mountain. The busiest mountain in Britain is Wales's Mount Snowdon, which has over 500,000 visitors every year. Amazingly, a railway can take tourists on a journey all the way to the **summit**.

Passengers on the Snowdon Mountain Railway make their journey to the top of the mountain.

Map of the UK

Here are the locations of the mountains and places mentioned in this book.

Glossary

abandoned deserted and left empty

abseiling dropping down a cliff face using a rope coiled around the body

adapted changed to suit the conditions

blizzard snowstorm with strong winds

camouflage hide by blending in with the surroundings

explosives materials that can be made to explode

destination place where someone goes

fertile able to produce lots of crops

glacier slow-moving mass of ice

miners workers who dig out coal or metals from the ground

molten molten describes rock that has turned into hot liquid

paraglider person who glides through the air on a wide parachute

peak pointed top of a mountain

range series of mountains found close together

resort place where many people go on holiday or take part in fun activities

scramble move across land using hands and feet

summit highest point of a hill or mountain

terrain land and its features

valley low area of land between the hills or mountains

vegetation plant life

volcano mountain or hill where molten rock and gas erupts through the surface

wingspan measurement across the wings from one wingtip to the other

Find out more

Books

Mountains (Geographywise), Jen Green (Wayland, 2014)

Mountains (Our Earth in Action), Chris Oxlade (Franklin Watts, 2014)

Rivers and Mountains, Joanna Brundle (Book Life, 2017)

Websites

www.bbc.co.uk/schools/gcsebitesize/geography/glacial_landscapes/
Glacial Landscapes and Processes: *Explore the effect glaciers have had on Britain's landscape.*

www.primaryhomeworkhelp.co.uk/mountains.htm
The Mountain Environment: *Information on how mountains form, and much more.*

Index

An Teallach 6, 30
animals 18

Ben Nevis 12, 14, 30
birds 19
Brecon Beacons 5, 22, 24

Cairngorms 14, 28, 30
caves 22
Cheviot Hills 5, 8
climbing 27
Cuillin 7, 30

Dartmoor 5, 21

farming 20, 21

glaciers 11

High Cup Nick 11, 30
Highlands 5, 6, 12, 14
hills 4, 5, 21

Lake District 4, 5, 13, 15, 25

mining 22
Mount Snowdon 13, 29, 30
mountain biking 26

Peak District 26, 30
Pen y Fan 24
Pennines 5, 11
Pistyll Rhaeadr 9, 30
plants 16, 17

quarries 23

railways 29
ranges 7, 14
rivers 4, 10

Scafell Pike 13, 30
ski resorts 28
Snowdonia 5, 10
soldiers 24
sports 28

tourists 21, 22, 26, 29

valleys 4, 9, 10, 11, 16, 20
volcanoes 7, 12

waterfalls 9
weather 15, 20, 21

Yorkshire Dales 20, 30